Trials Of A Stranger

Printed by: Great Unpublished Publishing

ISBN 1-58898-929-1

Manufactured in the United States of America

To get in touch with author go to
http://www.the_hood.com/members/poetry/nubian_poet/
or buy CDs "Trials Of A Stranger" or "Shedding My Skin"

email the author at deepcobra13@yahoo.com

Trials Of A Stranger

Mervyn R. Seivwright

greatunpublished.com
Title No. 929
2003

Trials Of A Stranger

Contents

The Author

Born in Dulwich, a suburb of London, England in 1970, Mervyn Richard Seivwright's, child hood started in Ipswich, Suffolk. He is the product of 2 Jamaican families that moved to England in the sixties. His early writing stated at the age of 14. At this point in his life he had already lived in Des Moines Iowa, Syracuse New York & was in Miami Florida. He never really had a stable foundation, thus putting his trust & feelings on paper. Due to traveling so much it opened his eyes to many situations, and environments that gave him the vision he has today. After high school, Mervyn attended the University of Tennessee in Chattanooga. There his work transposed & first became published giving the opportunity for his first stage reading, a positive impact to continue his writing.

This book, "Trials of a Stranger", is a door way to the many sides of Mervyn R. Seivwright. The title depicts the trials of his life. Describing life through the eyes of which he saw them. There are various styles of poetry shown in this book such as the cinquane called "The Jews", to the sonnet "Second Creepy Halloween Night". Much of the poetry here reflects many of his early works forming the basis to who he is today.

Trials of a Stranger

Everybody's life is full of mountains & valleys
Valleys & mountains... ...mountains & valleys
The struggle known is which stroke of the paintbrush will appeal to each
person we deal with
Is life the trials of law?
Not knowing the witness at the court door
Or knowing whom the jury is for
What sentence the judge will explore
Or is it the trials of time
Trials of time that string me out like a crack fiend
Trials that allow me to sing in joy
Maybe neither the fiend or joy, just experiences through time I employ
Choices that create my name
This is life, should I treat it as a game
Or as what... ... ...What I ask?
Well... ...you tell me,
My life has been a world of travel, but am I free
Or at least is my mind free
With my mind set free, I am free from all bonds
Free of the prisons that society places upon me
Family, work, the gridlock of the system that I see
Sometimes it seems like I am just running
Running, running and running
Running, running and running
Running with no rest for heavy eyes, heart, legs
I remember back playing with my cousins & friends
Endless play, endless fun, endless time
Time endless time... time endless time, time creped up on me

(Cont'd)

Time took me into the streets, hustling, observing, maintaining,
What it was to survive
Watching bullets fly
Tears for those who were murdered & died
For only inside I cried
Inside I cried
To show no fear, no pain, no weakness
In survival it was necessary for this
But this lifestyle I did dismiss
To the country... the south
Baby blue sky, mountains peaks drawn out the background far
Rich green valleys down below
Peaceful setting, real slow
Here I transitioned from my inner self
I left my mother's womb
I came to understand myself
Conformity was now assumed
Yes, I conformed
Handicapping my self expression, thoughts, ideas
Assimilating, never debating the society, work force, and environment to
which I am doomed
Stripped to bare nakedness of self
Re-clothed to foreign apparel, not even left with any self wealth
Will I be me again?
Me... will I be free, mentally again
Enough for you to know me
Have you ever known me?
Will you ever know me?
Do I know me?
I don't know
These are just the Trials of a Stranger

Mervyn R. Seivwright

The following poems are dedicated to, my Mother, the late Daphne Elora Seivwright (1950-1996). She made a lot of sacrifices to provide the best for her family. Not only did she work hard, she also taught us morals for a solid foundation in judgment and character to make a positive impact on those lives we touch.

Momma, I know you are watching over us from the Lord's hands since you were one of His soldiers, always seeking and following the light.

Bless You Momma...

November the Fourteenth

To this, my founder's day of birth.
I give to you, my love.
My focus now is just on you,
       Thou watch from up above.
I think of you in memories, in good & in bad too.
It was you alone, who help me see, the teachings of a man.
As I look back, I can now see, my head resting upon you.
Sometimes I feel lonely from your lack of presence, but there is one thing
       I can do.
I pray for comfort to understand life.
I pray for wisdom through.
I pray to hear your voice in my dreams,
       And strength you offer too.
I look into your eyes,
I see the friend, I see the joy, I see the you in me.
I shiver knowing that I must go on without the sight of thee.
Celebrate this day, your day, for in you is in me.
I hold you closely everyday, in my heart you see.
Tonight I light a candle bright,
       To warm the memories.
For in my soul, your shadow's cast inside eternally.
My mother I love you dearly,
       For this you've always known.
But I can go on joyfully,
       Because God has brought you home.

Momma

Momma, time left no time to spend on your day
Chaos has plagued me, 2 years has faded away
Is this what or must become of me?
I do not dream or seek to be happy
I feel I'm drained; my faith is not as strong
Careless, my heart, my soul is gone
I just live to see the next day
What's my desire in thee? I see dismay
It's not the end; it's just an endless path
I see its' movement, it's not going fast
I will go on, because I know that I should
My love for God that I know is always good.
Though I know He is not happy with my fall in grace
Others can't see, it's an internal face.
Momma, I ask you, what to do in time
I know with patience, yes He will provide.
Emptiness crawls my destined internal walls
My back is crooked I cannot stand too tall
The battle is against my own inner self
Momma this day, I wish to have your wealth
So much I see I missed, there was not time to learn.
But in God's plan, ready I was, I yearn
I feel the storms inside me corruptly explode
The sound of nails scraping on the blackboard, I feel the pain reload
I must stop, get on my knees, it's time for me to pray
In my mind & in my head, will this make me be okay?
Faith, I wish you find me if you can
Momma! Please help! Just once,
                    now that I am a man.

Trials
of
Images

An Image So Real To Me

In the eve, a second now, before the sunset falls
I start to see & hear a darkness inside, start to call
Like leprosy upon the skin,
A freezing chill, comes from within
As silence, feels the danger I meet
Where could I go, I was in too deep
I could hear the armies marching near
What in this darkness did I fear?
A pain that comes from no living man
Could I escape, even if I ran?
A tyrant, loud, such a thunderous cry
I must go on, my life to Him I deny
I feel the oceans, a blanket before me
10 feet in front, I can't even see
A light... a light is before me now
Such powers it has, should I just bow?
Hey! What is this? I am now in the light?
I tingling feeling, past pain, not in fright
I cannot feel my leg, to my dismay
The rain, thunder and lightning has called this my day
Do you see this storm where I endure injury?
A kiss so cold that hit my leg, and shocked my energy.
See the image that I have shown. To me it's just a dream,
Feeling a storm with no way out, no way to be redeemed

Desert Dreams

Mirages seen of home, lost in many minds
Foreign tongue, & a foreign look of many different kinds
Please don't use your life, to understand their own
Confusion misdirects you from a philosophy unknown
Look into the night, I see the desert shift
Lifeless 'till horizon, only stars do glow adrift
I dream to see the true unborn across the desert lie
Endless is the vision seeked; too soon the thirst does die
Images of dreams in mind do constantly reappear
Cold feelings waiting desperately beneath the flame to tear
Mental to the heart, does distant hold your soul
Time is the only battle, to watch the world unfold
Seek to see the motion, at early twilight
Watch to see the birds or prey for they are now at flight.

Everlasting Heavens

As we flew above the world so high
I was as a bird up in the sky.
Clouds of cotton float across the heaven like a quilted blanket.
Some clouds appeared as mountains and islands out of a sea of condensed air
Or a mist covering a lighthouse with rocks dangerous, but hard to see.
They are like ghosts drifting forever throughout time.
Solid to the eye.
Just a touch will transpose your mind into a lost dimension
An endless sea of clouds... Would it ever end?
Hold it!
I can't see anything.
The flight has ended.
Would tell you more, but that's another flight into your imagination.

What is Beauty?

What is beauty?
It is an unseen world beyond our fantasy.
Where all dreams can happen
Where nature lives forever without darkness falling upon it
With colors that are so many
The majority has not been named by man
And man can have immortal youth in this place I speak of
Then man can dance and play all through the day that never ends
Or just take a nap with the breeze chilling bumps upon your skin
While the hot sun glares into your face,
A tree suddenly appears to shield you
For just   the mere thought of anything in your mind can appear right
        before your sight.
But beauty to me is just one thing
        and that is to imagine what you desire.

Flower Internal

Do you see it? Never seen before...
Smell it, uncommon to me, yet I adore.
Touch it, velveteen so smooth
Taste it, like cotton candy sweet from my youth.
Color, shared from sky so high
Color, in the center of a sapphire's eye
Color, outlined silver as clouds drifting that you see
Color, that stems, through the valleys upon a blue mountain green
Flower, this is, before me now
Can you envision, will your mind allow?
Sacred, special, feel its grace.
A symbol of your soul, in a protected place.
Cherish this flower deep within you.
To feel your internal spiritual freshness with each morning dew.

Second Creepy Halloween Night

It was the day just before Halloween
And the evil was starting to clutter.
That night was the reign of the evil death queen,
At midnight she would fly and flutter,
As dark clouds cover the midnight sky
The full moon appeared like the world's end
Blocked out by evil the stars just passed by
I cried in fright, for death was not my best friend
Halloween's last second had passed again
And the evil of the world broke loose
As witches and Goblins moved around bends
Blood crept down the walls like raspberry juice
Then at a door, a kid said, "Trick or Treat"
Then POW! Like a flash, he and doom would meet.

Use Your Heart

Use your heart & not your eyes
In a dream you fantasize,
Imagery yet to unfold,
Of the feelings seen & not told
See a Pegasus in flight,
Black as coal, filled with inner might
Draws upon the soul on one,
A Unicorn, from where life begun
Families of two are distance past
One soaring high, one with nature's grass
To be filled with the joy of a union of two
Leaves memories the heart cannot elude
Elegance of the Pegasus & Unicorn,
Only tend to touch the dreaming
Understand the message of elegant,
Just know the dream's end & true meaning.

Lost Horizons

As the sun sets, spirits enter the air
The sun is half seen over the horizon
Flames of a fire are seen over the water
Making a path to a lost world
Dwelled by only the eternal spirits of feelings
Where love is gracious
Where sadness leads to sorrow
But hate is overseen and has minor qualities
Where life is eternal only through the heart, not from the mind
Where honor is your story and life
And those that make the trip will transpose to a spirit made of their heart
And will never be seen or return again because
He will be in the lost world of the unseen horizon.

The Seas of Cotton

As I look across the sky I see
A sea of pearl white cotton reaching out to the horizon.
Ready to catch me if I should fall.
Holding me like being in my mother's arms.
The sun drifts its cry as it reaches across the horizon with its' radiant red glow.
Shifting winds change their emotions and
Stretch across the vast scenery that is consistently changing.
But on this day it gives the enlightenment of shifting into a New World.

Trials
Of
Love

Valentyne Dai

Now it's time, in early spring.
With the world of wings it shall begin
To choose what destiny has foreseen
A sacred emotion, to share without sin.

A day before Lupercalia,
A great love feast, a pagan day.
Named after 1, or 3 before, the year 300 AD
On February the 14th, in early martyrology.

Saint Valentyne's, oh Valentines,
That's what we call it now.
Is it too commercial?
Lacking loves true vows?

Love, a word, that captures all,
      Given to us by God
We take time now,
      One day it is for all our love, how odd.

Be sincere, for love untrue, will loose it's meaning here.
Your feelings should channel endlessly all throughout the year.
Focus on this day, the real deep throbbing thirst inside
What modern day has accepted for us with a wall to hide.

Are we very shallow, & really seek the facts?
You'll always feel the emptiness that comes from false love acts.
Open the well, so deep & cold.
Let the truth be known
So you   can reflect, on Valentine's Day,
And the love that with your mate has grown.

I Show You Me

As we jump across the rod of life, to be joined eternally.
Our partnership is bonded by the thoughts that we cannot see.
Communicate & trust in thee, show faith in what we know.
Life is now for us, not them, to share our lives & show.
Show the battles internally that we solely wish to fight.
Show the images of dreams that build up inner might.
Show the past of joys & falls that made us who we are.
To show is important what's inside so our minds will not go far.
Images tell many stories different to you & me.
What you feel from an image, the other may not see.
Time can be a precious thing, take the time to know.
Communicate & understand, then in time, your love will grow.

The Romantic Zone

When we dwell in this zone words are not spoken.
This is an image I thought I'd never see
In this surrounding I use all my senses.
Let me tell you what I feel and see.
Darkness of sky, with stars showing great depth wishing that one of the
stars feels your dreams.
Clouds drifting by as they are blown by the west wind appear as ghost birds
just flocking by.
I see two thirds of the moon peering yonder for it is the only headlight of
this midnight sky.
Palm trees swaying to a breeze that dances on our skin
It's not cold because she is right in my arms keeping me warm.
Sand feels so soft beneath my feet
Do you know where I'm at right now?
Don't move till you see the whites of their eyes.
It's just the waves just crashing on the shore constantly until out of sight.
It's like your heart just driving onward looking for the unseen with the
feeling there.
Though my eyes have the glory & she is holding me right here.
Quiet so quiet, is it right now all except that water sound.
I get a feeling it's so perfect so it cannot last that long
When the great Chariot of Apollo rises, the romance mist of the night is
gone.
Cherish this moment and never forget for time goes on to past.
Since memories can never die then in my heart you'll stay.
For this night on the beach was a dream I always had.
To share with a lady that's only true.
Thank you, good night and remember as I leave you before first light.

What First Comes To Mind

Your question was, "What is the first thing that comes to mind?"
Like clouds making a quilt blanket of a quiet breezy night.
Like mountains high up in the clouds where my mind drifts gazing right at you.
Like the rivers that pierce the land guiding one heart to you.
With many things upon my mind,
The first thing that comes is you.
There's a lot I don't understand too,
But the Lord still works for me.
While I draw you into my arms we'll share our faith in He.
We will share the problems and share the fun
And grow to make our world become one.
I do not think, I just write,
What is the first thing that comes to mind?

A Silent Face

Silence is a silent face
What are the words when our eyes embrace?
It seems like our souls in time were to meet
Though verbal silence will come to defeat
This is what I sense from my heart about you
A women of class, frail and sensitive too
Beauty from within, that glorifies through
As I put my head down,
I pray, "Lord what should I do?"
Fill me with wisdom, in heart and in mind
Give me the knowledge so I can provide
The words so sincere, for the lady before me
Her presence... an aura that I cannot describe in thee
It makes me feel strangely, it's good without answer
Pour out your essence, in my hand at this time
For it is so precious for deep understanding
So I won't seek darkness, but in your heart, a light I'll find
To lead me onward in the right direction
Then you can receive my honest affection
A man of sensitivity you will find
Behind the words in my quiet mind.

Love, My heart

What is love?
A gust of shivers running through my body
I wish I could touch it
It's too far away
I can hear it
I can feel it
But, mile-by-mile it cuts with pain
I cannot breathe
It flows
But grows with intensity as each second goes by
Fireworks pierce, deep, flaming blood to my heart
She was so close, but so far away
Now she is far away, but so close
I ponder about you
You see visions of me
Please reality, set me free
Soul to soul
Just right
Look into her eyes and remember how
If love is like this, it's not a mistake
Why? Why?
   So far away, time goes slow
                           Just wait! I'll see you soon
My flower, my precious one, my Love
My heart

The Light Deep Inside

Back & forth time is endlessly seeking no end
As my soul travels within its outskirts
As to my heart has been a pulse to the deaf
A resonance of light has traveled depths,
Multiple to the Labyrinth
Lord spread this light across the world for it is wedged inside ready for...
I don't know, I just feel the dawn as a gift,
Presented in my hands with a golden sense.
Though more precious than Gold
To loose it, I loose the beauty, so I closely hold,
And feeling a life form abstract of that conformed
I have opened up my heart for you, come here and
Dwell to share the beauty, the caring and sharing
Let our souls become one
As that, in which flies of the fire, the Phoenix
We must enter into the flame, a rebirth.
Just a light, a feeling, an emotion
                    A tear
                        A smile
                            You
                                The light

Trials
of
Society

Summertime Flow

Eyes closed,
Rustling wind
Waves crashing, with a sting
Sounds of seagulls fight at flight
Searching, rumbling, for one small bite
Children's voices scream at play
BBQ, Smoking, mouth watering today
Radio fades to distant skies
I feel the heat of a sun so high
Dominoes hit the table,
Competition must be deep
Women close in gossip, about people from last week
As I lay upon the substance, which is soft & unstable be
Let your eyes remain closed, use your senses & see the vision I see
Small engine plane is flying low
Or helicopter rides, showing scenes from below
Heat has cooled, body is now drained
The sense that the sunset must be wrapping up the day
I feel a little hand rubbing me to & fro
Eyes open,
My daughter's face tired,
"Daddy, I am ready to go."

The Roar of the Crowd

As the final minutes came before the gates were opened
And the fear of the crowd aroused me,
Then that second ticked off
As if it was an army, marched in, but with large, harsh voices,
Insulting and taking out those traitors among them.
Was the world at war?
It felt that way, but it was only a football game
But was it only a football game?
No, it was a grand finale.
Life savings were expressed in bets
For we were the underdogs but consider this,
Maybe we were the underdogs,
But we never went under for we were victorious.

Written in 1985 at the Miami Dolphins and Chicago Bears football game at
the Orange Bowl
Stadium in Miami FL. This was the one blemish in Chicago's championship
season.

Music Man

Before I go
I have to tell you a couple of things,
About a music man who loves to sing.
He plays a keyboard, a drum, and a sax,
So watch out for his jazz attack.
He plays around the world just for fun,
And has free concerts, so you ought to come.
When he leaves the scene you hear a little muffle,
And then a small song, a little mist, and finally nothing...

Time is Crystal Clear

I look into the crystal & what do I see
Time's pathway must be clear in front of thee
Time can be your friend
Time can drag you down
Time, you either master or it masters you around
As time leads you to leave
Was the time a stepping-stone?
This time is yours, a time to grow
To make the time your own
Time will not stand still, waiting on your name.
This is your time to make a stand,
A catalyst for change.

Who Decides?

How can you call me white or black?
When to my Lord I'm just another soul.
He takes me for my mind deep inside and for where heart and feelings go.
You call me black by the color of skin,
       but some call me white from the content within.
So tell me please, how can you tell the color of a person from the content inside?

If I'm white and I act black I speak a broken English,
I'm inclined to be a criminal, and my attitude is bad.
If I'm black and I act white, I'm accepted because I'm good.
I speak the proper English, and don't hang out in black neighborhoods.

Stereotypes lead this speculation for you judge the color of skin.
For we are all individuals, and bodies are composed of similar things.
It's you, the environment that set the standard,
       and to the selfishness of race no one is right.
But with knowledge you loose your ignorance,
       and the stereotype is a lost belief.
Take away the color of skin in mind at thought,
       and put in the stereotypes from which you were taught.
Too many will not fall within their race,
       and you will see that this isn't a white & black place.

Trials
of
Blackness

Born Black, Die Black

Born to a color of mystery.
It wasn't my choice,
Seemed like just another color to me.
So why do I feel a negative burden?
I soon start school to learn,
Just to hear a nickname stowed upon me.
I don't understand, was I any different?
For the first time I notice my skin color is not the same.
Am I not human?
There is only one or two of us here.

Well time answers all questions.
What is the answer time?
Why is it that the law says that we are treated equal?
but really in the souls of the lawmakers we are not.
Why is it that we understand unity is the answer to success,
but really we understand and destroy each other anyway.
Why is it that we know knowledge is the key to the future,
but really money & power are dominant in the heart for now.
Why are we listed as a general stereotype,
but really we are individuals in the same world.

I will soon die **Black**,
and time leaves many unanswered questions.
Do you want to wait for time?
or can you find the answers for the questions seen and untold.
So why is it that you listen with pride and eagerness,
but really you to are waiting on time and die with the unanswered
question...
Why is that?

African Princess

The inheritance is yours, woman of color, filled with spirit.
I feel the roar of your fire.
Blessed with natural curves & a passionate soul.
Features distinct of African birth right
Too blessed, to share the image that the media seeks.
I feel your inner drive to succeed
So much pride you should possess
Show me your royalties, the princess that you are
Respect, Dignity, Wisdom & Heart,
The base of a Sapphire beginning to shine
You are deep-rooted, fierce to unkind
Sensitive internal, sharing only with those that share your plight
I wonder for you what plagues your mind
The supply of the African Prince is a lacking list for you
Many of my brothers seek to descend in the eves of self-destruction
Or find slavery from a master that whips their inner will
Only you in the presence of my Lord,
Can break this trend, my African Princess
My Princess
It's time that you smile,
And let your joy gleam in the sunlit sky
Heavy has been your burden
My Lord let's me share that weight
I feel the pain,
From the beatings mentally that our society has placed upon you
But you have and always will prevail
Last, I pray that you bloom as in early morn as does a rose,
Spreading its beauty to the world
I pray that you remember from whence you came
I see the sparkle in your eye
That penetrates the soul,
That fills us full of energy, a power to unfold
The time is now, my Princess
From you, in which the world has came
Now it's time to flourish and to be that Queen again.

Do you see me?

Is your heart with me?
I cannot represent myself
I need attention, love & affection
I don't do much now, but show love
I am warm & cuddly, giving you moments of joy
My real mother is too young to raise me.
Can you adopt me?

Can you be patience with me?
I am fun & full of energy
I'll play any game or sport, take me anywhere
I just started the 3rd grade
My mom, she works all the time,
& my father, my mom said he was important,
But I never knew him
I wait at the Boy's Club for positive motivation away from the streets
Will you volunteer?

Do you feel my joy?
It's finally over, graduation day.
I'm cultured, educated, and full of new ideas.
For you, I will achieve to help you fly higher than you demand
I have worked hard these past 22 years.
Graduating Suma Cum Laud, to let you know I mean business.
May I seek employment with you?

Do you remember me?
I am full of wisdom, experience, & knowledge.
I loose feelings in my body here & there.
All my family has moved away.
It's a quiet world, by myself
I miss the sounds of laughter & play
Boy, that seems like it was just yesterday.
Do you have time to visit with me?

You see us everyday,
Some even mirror your lives
We are a people seeking other,
Though our life battles go through strife.
The only things that different, our image is black you see.
Why should it even matter since were all in God's family

Wake Up Your Mind!

"Wake up",
I said, "WAKE UP?"
I ask,
Do you see?
        Do you feel?
                Or do you show,
RACISM?
Are you blind?
Or think it no longer exists?
You are naive, in a game where I am the piece left out
You'll never know unless you bear my color of skin
Did you wish to care, or understand my true despair?
Did you feel my cries, a waterfall of silent tears inside?
For this I must always hide
Because I fear the sword, that strikes the weakness in me
Are you insensitive, though you've never known?
You never cared to ask... You just say...
"I am always nice"; "I have done no wrong"
Friends of color have you
Could they call you friend at all?
Do you even know their blues?
It's time for you to understand
In looking at the color of skin,
And what the hatred of it can do
Or are you that read this, the one that I must face
That wishes of my demise, since I am not of your race
You don't have a love for God, or you would seek to love all
Because of your hatred, it will lead to your downfall
Again, I ask you to "wake up", "WAKE UP!"
The problem is now.
If you cannot reach out, or think I speak not to you
You will succeed as the issue,
Now, in my eyes, just what would you do?

Brother Man-Brother Man

Brother man, young black man I say.
Living a life filled with nothing but games.
Have you any morals, or live for no reasons.
Life to you may seem like a sexual season.
Money is important to you.
At the expense of your brother man too.
Sex is something, just to do you see.
It's just like Russian roulette with different chambers to me.
A chamber, you lucky and got yours here.
A chamber of birth and the choice is there.

> To take responsibility is the right thing to do.
> Though responsibility is a word you wish to screw.
> Guidance is not there for a newborn life.
> It may die soon or be a youth in fright.

Don't feel guilty, there's chambers left.
Though these are the chambers that may lead to death.
A chamber of gonorrhea, a shot can cure you of the burning urine.
A chamber of syphilis, which is worse than chamber three
A chamber where a condom was good to you.
A chamber of AIDS where your life is through.
Think through these chambers and then you'll see
That sex is overrated & there is more to life.
Unless you already know the lady who will be there to be your wife.
The next problem here is drugs on the street.
You either kill someone here, or your death you'll meet.
It's not a black man's fault why drugs are here.
Though we are the one's dying from year to year.
The boats & planes owners, it's not us you see.
To ship it into the GHETTO is another creed's kill plea.
We don't make guns, though we have them all.
Killing each other till our race does fall.
Please think my brother and rise to an education.
Learn about your race and give positive vibrations.
It's we the young black male, the image to lead.
And don't forget GOD,

> because it was our people that he freed.

Read about the people that lived in that time.
Even Moses was like Egypt, in the color of skin tone.
And Egypt was of the Black Man, with their face upon the throne.
These are the facts.

> You may read them again.
> > It is now up to you,

> > > Young Black Man,
> > > My Friend.

Forty Acres & A Mule

40 years, the time has come.
I see a pretty green
Fertile land, to grow some crops, I can't believe the scene
For all the pain that we have felt,
And all our kinfolk cries.
The bloodshed on three of four sons, why did they have to die?
Reconstruction was the word,
A joy, it was something good.
We reconstructed everything,
Negroes couldn't even get any wood.
That president tried to free us slaves,
But all of us weren't set free.
Not for two more years in 1865, Jun 19th it would be.
They told us they would pay us,
For the human rights crimes to be erased.
It took 40 years, of sweat & tears to finally win my cased.
Forty Acres & A Mule, I won, finally something that is mine.
With you my dear, I hold you close, my God we hold divine.

"40 acres & a mule came in heaven's paradise; for the old promise stayed
broken, with a continuing price".

Why are we so Cruel?

Why are we so cruel?
Close your eyes right before me
So you can clearly vision what I see
What stops us from unity, the dreams, lost in the community?
Who stops us, a question you ask?
Why are we so cruel?

Looking down the daylight streets
Weaving, bobbing just to meet
The prey to settle in their trap
2 eight-year-old boys are selling smack
The time is fall... kids are in school
The drug pusher uses kids as fools
Why are we so cruel?

A young family just received a loan
To start a store in their neighborhood home
They wish to dedicate these things for free
Money, time & supplies, for a center to be
On the night they first opened, a gunshot rang
The wife lays bloody, husband cries in her hand
Why are we so cruel?

Mr. Jones a CEO, successful as the title shows.
Must hire a partner for his firm, so listen the facts he knows.
One black, one white, Mr. Jones a black man too.
The young black man is more qualified, quick choice, what would you do.
The young white man will get the job, the president guarantees
For a vice president job Mr. Jones will get, all he must do is agree.
He's happy with the golden rule.
To succeed at all cost, he thought was cool
Why are we so cruel?

Why are we so cruel, to us, a people seeking unity?
We tunnel out the outside letters, & the "I" has set us free
Keep your eyes close, the image is you, "I'm not cruel", you say
How many times have you said "I" to earn your position today?
Each time you do resort to "I", you regress the community
Open your eyes, see the light, & know your position here.
To teach, show, & practice against the cruel acts our people share.

A Good Black Man

A Good Black Man
Future Father, Husband and Head of Family
Responsible, Respectable, Caring
Understanding Pride, Distinction and Honor
Cultural, Strong
God First

Is this right & hard to find
Should all black males be of this kind?
A few to the world,
That's what we're told
Due to death, prison, and drugs that are sold.

Though, what makes you worthy dear ladies I see?
For ladies are many, but few good to me
Can you be picky, bossy or rude?
For you bad, and him good is rather crude
Don't be defensive, for you I don't hate
Just don't take for granted a man you wish to dictate
For what a man gives, he must also receive
And be in God's blessing, so you will be pleased

Unless you aren't ready, and wish for no good
For this, that I explained, you've never truly understood
Because you challenge man with issues or compromise your wants
With the ego or an ignorant man
And then with your friends that name is taught
Dog to the guy you challenged, that beat you every time
Dog was the generalization to all guys on your mind
So ask yourself the question,
Are you ready for a good black man this time?

Black Women

Hello black women, if I must say
So proud of your color on this very day.
Full of culture & life, it makes me just dream
You came so well packed, so special you seem.
Not dirty, cruel, stingy or mean,
       Not dishonest, spoiled, or live for negative things.
Full of ideas, deep in heart, and good for the race.
Come now & help me in this growing place.
As our minds form into one.
Each thought endures to grasp the sun.
Through stars piercing onward in the night.
In vast space searching endlessly for the light.
That light, Oh Light!
      For what Malcolm X screamed,
           The Black Panthers fought,
                And Dr. King dreamed.
Help me black women & be my joy.
For you are the one that gives me hope.
Black unity must be strong right now to cope.
Not black on black crime,
      But black on black caring.
Taking a step to succeed where we may.
If I lost my direction & lost my sight.
You would be the Black Women to help me find
                   The light.

This is My Community

Back in 1964 we were a clan in a common war.
We knew as one, we could open doors.
We had marches, meetings & different boycotts.
A community together we were a power non-stop.
Not violence, but wisdom would educate our minds.
We knew that ignorance was not the answer in the baffle cry.
As we transition onward, times were yet to change.
In time we saw leaders killed, who took us from whence we came.

The seventies were a break down of the decade before.
Drugs & guns were germs implanted in our community war.
Germs for money, germs for power, and superficial things.
Little was the growth, but then in time the germs grew wings.
Riots surfaced in the air, though positive...were they?
The community suffered viciously, for it was self inflicted pain.

As I seek the present now, the wounds of past are here.
You will see the contrast, from the last 20 years.
This is not about steps, that one or two have made.
In government, sports & other things from the investment the community
                                        paid.
We look at the community where our future laid.
Where the germs of past are stronger, controlling our own lives.
Germs that control the colors, that our children wear every day.
Germs of weed & crack cocaine, and keep the streets from play.
Germs of incarceration, not the way you see.
The bars are now invisible, around the community.

This is my community, and aware I make you now.
You know of the past baffles, and yet you wonder, how?
How and what can I do to be a soldier in the streets?
The young must see the role models of positivity.
Cultivate & educate with time, the difference you will see.
But if you loose the time to invest,
                    We will lose our community.

Trials
of
Remembrance

In Memory of James Byrd Junior of Jasper Texas

As I look down

As I look down,
I thank the lord for sparing me to peace
As I look down,
I got to see my body on the street
As I look down,
My feelings are real mixed, not pure
As I look down,
What had I done, a torn up corpse, that seemed like a settled score
As I look down,
Joy misunderstood the images of their face
As I look down,
I felt their souls & I couldn't feel disgrace
As I look down,
Could hatred of my race cause this bloody mangled scene?
As I look down,
No justice is fair, only through the Lord will justice be redeemed
As I look down,
I see the tears that flood the eyes that weep for me.
As I look down,
Don't shed your tears, from racism, I am set free.
As I look down,
I see the country, shocked in every place
As I look down,
You don't see the others that were killed from present hate for my race.
As I look down,
I see the loud talking, but the youth need action for a future free.
As I look down,
Just one more time, I leave this question on your mind.
When will race just be left out?
And judge me for my inner self
Are you scared to face true me?
Feed your lack of knowledge,
And then you will be set free.

The Jews

The Jews
Died for unjustly
Flames scorched their skin to Ash,
Screaming and burning, though they live,
Angels

Ronnie's Cry

I need a liver.
And I need it really bad before I cry and start to die.
I have to find one now.
Just show me how.
I'm 7 years old.
I need time to grow.
I, Ronnie DeSillers.
I just need my 4th liver and I hope to adjust
for that is a must.
I want to be like you and do what kids do
I need a liver today
If I enter heaven real soon
I'll leave my love in my last room.
For I remember the love you gave me.

ALEX

I'm going to write a poem for you
About a boy with pride, and talent too.
He passed away on the seventh of February
For a stupid reason that wasn't very merry.
He motivated me, and many more.
And helped an organization that he believed for.
He wrote poems like I do, to express his heart
About his girlfriend and problems that fell apart
In the kingdom of God is where he now lies
But God has told me his last thoughts before he said goodbye.
Dear Shannon, I'm still here & love you
And to the band, get a superior for me like you should do
I've prayed for him each and every day
For a boy that was a friend, but in a special way
His name is Alex Gutierrez
And in our hearts he'll stay

Trials
from
Internal

Seer of Minds

A reflective glass over a well so deep
Can it reflect and also keep
The contents, so sensitive & frail
If they are split it can share your tale
As I peer in your looking glass
I see black holes in thee
Some are void of shape & form
Others try to redirect my beam
I see the inner soul to trust
I feel the pain, blunt, dark, & cold
I hear your vibration of your mind
Like a seer of your soul
I don't know why I have this gift
I don't seek this in me
God has blessed me, to penetrate
To understand from underneath thee
It is not a game that I do quest
I quench nor thirst nor desire
When you present & show yourself
You'll bring your inner fire
Infinity it will burn in you
The well won't put out the flame
Don't try to disguise, what will never leave
Your internal branded name.

A Hand in a Glove

A hand in a glove, or is it a myth
Four fingers & a thumb have symbolized a philosophy once missed
A Sense of a deep admiration, a quest from in a desert lies
Searching endlessly to find that one jewel of the Nile.

One, two, three, four, five the count, the middle I'll start with first
Finger in the middle, nasty to others, but yet I found its thirst.
In the middle I do find, the attribute that touches minds.
A mental stimulation this is true, though equal minds can conquer through

Between the center & the thumb, comes the deep intelligent one
To understand the knowledge here, can you grasp it? Can you share?
Shallow was the game once played, but oceans are my field today.

Between the middle & pinkie shown misunderstandings from emotion
                              groans.
A treasure box, we keep beneath, to share it, do you think your wealth will
                              cease.
A fragile part, which won't declare, does it shatter year to year?
Control it & your fear will be, a surge of strength internally.

Now what easy is the thumb, it is different representing fun.
Humor is a quality extreme, with the others, it make a balanced team.

Almost last, the pinkie one, too many say it's great, overrated by this one.
Physical expression is what I see, with blinded eyes, physical can't be.
Physical view & physical felt, are things that lack pure joy.
A vision touch by objects inanimate, though the main hand is not
                              employed.

Most important, the guardian, that shields us day by day.
He's the leader that I must follow, the glove, the only way.
The faith I have in Jesus Christ protects the elements here.
He is the balance, the love & joy,
          The hand in the glove I share.

Do You Know the Clown?

Look at the Clown's face, and see the shear delight
Joy to the children gives them smiles so bright
Tear away the makeup & look into the eyes
Seeking deep inside **himself,** you feel the long silent cries
Play the game of life, just to be the same
Reform, conform, do as you're told and society will claim.
Is that how it is? Or how it is to be?
The truth of the clown, there is no respect in being **he**
He has become   an expression, not of **himself** but what society has
                    molded
He feels trapped inside **himself** like in prison walls his feelings are cold
One final tear we come when society looses its use for **him**
And the one time individual **he** was, is forever lost within
What is the direction, blinded there's no sight
The show is over, the clown is gone, **he** is faded into the night.

Light of Life

I want to see the light of life
I want to see the dream
I want to see the body felt from deep within the seams
I want to see the heritage of a rare one true
I want to see a part of me but what am I to do

I seek to understand & know the thought that others see
I seek to understand that if there is a quest on me
I seek to understand & view the plans the Lord has made
I seek to understand inside, have all my debts been paid
I seek to understand that why the soul of one can let me see the pain

I look for wisdom to the one that guides me everyday
I look for trust from deep inside from what others say
I look for peace down in the heart a resonance unsure
I look for the joy of unique touch just like one time before
I look for endless inspiration from a flame beneath the core

I want, I seek, I look for one, desires are now here.
In your eyes as your read this know you feel what I hold dear
A life, a life is what is there, small, but grand to me
Please feel my tears, a deep ravine, that pours so endlessly

Curiosity

Curiosity starts at the sight of you
Observing every actions, words, and expression
Suspicions, conclusions, wonder the unknown thoughts you hold
How you think, what you think, seeking the true personality.
How deep is your mind & heart of deepness of your spiritual soul?
Curiosity filled in my mind with your humorous thoughts silent to the
               world
Are you like Pandora's box or are you a nice surprise
Only time will know & show the essence, which you do hide
You are unique, a delicacy unknown.
Curiosity builds up, though in time I'll know you well.
You are of an interesting nature not hard to tell.
This was written directly to you.
Not to talk, give lines, just as real as I can be
It is for the curiosity I have of your expressions deep in your face.
Yes, you've kept me thinking that I must say.
For my Lord has blessed you in a special way.

Mirror Dimension

As I look deep into a mirror of dimensions
It gives a 3 dimensional image to what I see
It also tells much more
But only from with me
For when I speak it simulates,
The sounds and movements made
To learn the knowledge of the mirror,
The first place I must look is here

Here is me, inside myself
Here I find the dream
Here is where the image starts to duplicate the scene

So let appear my feelings here, what I wish to see
Emotional, physical, intellectual, and mental
Forms of stimulation that comes from inside of me
What I wish to see is a motion I must make
To make the mirror image perfect, is what the dimension will take
Everyday in my mind, I think of this mirror
Understanding, I'm the source of the dimension to thee
I'll take a chance to give this what is boiling inside me
And if the mirror is really there
I'll receive what I give of me.

Untruths

Eyes can tell A million tales, except the soul within.
About a tale of a world so gold, or lead from beneath.
The waves of water...steady flow, without a sense of end.
The direction is an emotion felt, but quickly it can pretend.
Powerful & weak, it may be, but constant the cascade.
Control them and the force will fall,
Let them loose the world will call.
Is there a way I can maintain & understand the secrets that are so deep?
Hear them, though to communicate they cannot do.
See them, though you can only envision your own thoughts.
Touch them, though it feels so cold with a pseudo confidence too.
Trust them, though it's time to question what a wave's feeling will do.
Let's look deeper down inside, to the undertow beware.
It's shifting winds from down below, to protect secrets not to share.
Unsteady is the secrets' vortex, so with caution, it won't prevail.
So are the waves you see so steady? Will you know their tale?
Action, reaction, you thought you knew.
The world is deeper than your mind, or to where your thoughts will go.
Only your soul can penetrate, if steady like the waves.
This alone you can maintain, true in soul, so that the waves will be tamed.

Spread My Wings

Spread my wings, long, high, lost in an unseen world,
Floating endlessly across a path of crystal clouds.
My mind is so free, no bonds, just emptiness.
What am I missing? I have my Lord & me.
I can feel a glowing energy within my soul.
Could it be the prison of my heart?
For thoughts that have truly seen deep inside I know it's pure,
          though few have knowledge.
Is there any escape for my heart?
Is anyone there to hear?
Am I in this world forever?
Beauty or material form, are not the successors of this quest
It is of the mind, the heart and the soul within the Lord.
Is life too real to seek this I ask?
Please give me strength within your great wisdom
As I fly, I see rivers of gold & riches of unbelief
But the most precious thing to me is the freedom,
          and free flow of my soul, which feels trapped like in a Labyrinth
Only finding dead end walls.
Outside, joy is but a step away,
          Inside I feel the cold air blowing & decaying.
My heart is pure, but slowly going.
If you are, I mean, be you pure too.
          Save me, before it is not I you feel.
Time has dreams of changing senses.
Yours is the last for hope,
          or this world will be my home.

Trials
of
Sorrows

Me

I am the moon
Alone and cold
In a misdirected desolate place.

I am lost
Within myself
Unable to find whom I am

I am a disease
A bad influence
That spreads the world

I am dead
Through reality's
Unrealistic world

I am a wandering spirit
Traveling through time and dimension
Unable to take to anything

Now, who am I to you?

The Prison In Me

Lord, please hear me, what I now tell
Free me from this prison cell
Time has priced an agony
I want to welcome victory
Cold & desolate are these walls
Blood stains, deep about me crawls
Beating, torture, were the cause
Thinking of this makes me pause
Is this my punishment? I ask.
I try my best on every task
Expectation from we, I can't fulfill
This is why now, I am ill willed
So now I deserve a secluded place
To hide the image, called my face
Though, no one who came remembered me
Within, A stranger I've always been
The flesh they saw, a shallow tale
Was the only thought, they wish would fail
You never saw the me in you
Life's presence made your environment too
I wish, a moment you seek out me
Then the depth of pain could set me free.
Free...I see an unknown light
Free...To taste inner glory delight
Free...To run to distance lands
Free...To touch slowly your gentle hands
Free...To hear thoughts of minds' true
Free...I could be, just feel me right through
I ask you to look at the prison in me
A second of patience, see in Me and I'll be FREE

"LIFE"

It hurts again, yes that is true
But is there anything that I can do?
I feel a dreaded pain,
Like a dull dagger filled with black blood entered my soul.
Making it feel shivering and cold
Ready to blow away at any time.
I knew what would happen
History repeats itself
And my lessons are never learned.
It's almost like smoking, a bad habit
You're always trying to quit but you hear a voice inside say,
"Just one more time!"
And "Boom!"
It hurts again, yes that is true
But is there anything that I can do?

Behind Closed Doors

I'm lonely on the floor,
         But behind closed doors.
I'm subjected to rejection,
         Society's made it's own selections.
This is not my time you see,
         This part of my life is too hard for me.
Why do I treat myself this way?
         I destroy my heart and soul each day.
The strange feeling of my past ideas,
         Ring like a ghost throughout my ears.
I don't understand,
         So for my life I now band
My love,
         My hope,
                 And my heart.

The Subject is You, the Environment

Thy mind is dull and heart is cold
In my life at only 20 years old
I know myself not for wants & needs
Only the black blood in my soul to believe
I have no problem from what I now see
I'm just a subject of the environment in front of me
If I do fail there can be no worries
I do what you tell me, and success is a how
I am a scapegoat, or individual for frustration
My environment labeled this role to my life now
Laughing and jokes can be taken so far
Because of my differences, things I do, you do hate
Sympathy I ask not, for you're, your own problem
For you understand not, the support to my case
Who makes you the judge? When you did not make me.
And don't give me any denial, with the guilty look on your face
I do not care, for your words are meaningless
For I subject myself to the pain of disgrace
I live in limbo, out of reality's arm reach
I am a subject of society's bad taste
I have no glory; chills come to thought, to what you've got
I'm finished in that,
               that I thought was right
For I am just a brain and I've ended the fight.

Trials
of
the
Lord

Agape Love

Do you love my Christ?
Can He love you too?
Do you ever ask yourself, "What Would Jesus Do?"
Is it just in public where you share the life He gave
But when you are in private, you have brought shame to his name
Are your inner thoughts, as pure as they should be?
If not, let those tears fall, and ask to repent for thee
Do you have a hatred, or bitterness on your heart?
The Lord cannot reach you, until your inner anger will part
Are all of your burdens heavy, just to hard to take?
Think, "What am I doing?" just give Him the weight
Christ loves you always, unless you think He's not real
Agape is the loves he shares
A love you'll always feel
Do you feel deserving?
To receive such a love for you
Maybe it's time to fall on your knee & be forgiven
So in Him you can be renewed.
Agape Love...

Could He Walk With You

If He was beside you, could you still be you
If He could just read your mind, would your thoughts be true
If you walked together, think of these things that I say
Before you start to ask yourself, "Am I ready today?"
Does He approve of your friends?
Does He approve of your language?
Does He believe of your trust in thee?
Your attitude at home, job, leisure and church
Would He be pleased with what he sees?
Would He desire, to have you as a friend?
And say you remind Him of He
In your everyday life right now answer these questions for me
What would you show Him?
Where would you take Him?
Who would you let meet Him?
Why is it, I ask
You aren't walking with the Lord?
If you're not striving inside, outside you wear His mask
The Lord is next to you,
Even if you don't see Him
He is watching everything you do

Loneliness to Man

Standing by myself in a lonely world.
It happens all the time to boys and girls.
Then I draw myself to one hope.
Where I keep my faith and in my heart I promote.
The Father, Son, and the Holy Ghost.
For spiritual friend he gives the most.
Loneliness is produced from a sense of no common bond.
From past or present, likes or where you come from.
You feel the environment is wrong, which you start to hate,
But there's no reason to run, don't even escape.
You don't have to run if you're in the Lord's name.
Your faith in him will make that common bond the same.
When things look rough and don't start good,
There is something that's always misunderstood.
If you call on him things will work out.
If you work, keep your faith, and don't let your mind have doubt.
Partners and companions are really not needed.
Nice to have, but many times misled
Unless your mind is strong,
Then you keep your morals and it doesn't lead you wrong.
This is hard to do, so get a hand from God.
Everyday in your life,
            in the light,
                    under the sun.
Just pray and have your blessings there.
You will never again be lonely because you'll have Him that cares.

Let Me Fall In Grace

I forgot the prayer in me now.
That keeps me going and shows me how.
To take the world through you in grace.
So I don't fall in your disgrace.
I see myself through hope.
You gave me the experience in wisdom to cope.
The growing feeling here must come.
When I clear my heart and mind to one.
Show me desires to share your work and glorify the souls within.
I look one more time right into the light for the time of revelations is
   coming near.
Remember your heart's last desire for Jesus will overcome.

Acknowledgment

Dear Lord,
I pray that what you have blessed me to write is laid upon the hearts of those that read.
I thank you for allowing me to be one of your children.
My past has molded me through the trials I have endured.
In your eyes I understand that my continuous growth
Is necessary to properly give testimonies that are real to those that I interact with.
I thank you for praising me with a mother that gave me the tools to love you
And share your gift with others.
Amen.

Mervyn R. Seivwright